■ WAR VEHICLES ■

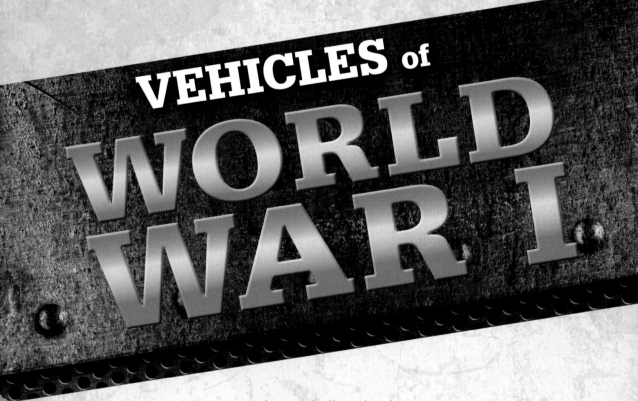

# VEHICLES of WORLD WAR I

by Michelle Schaub

Consultant:
Dennis P. Mroczkowski
Colonel, U.S. Marine Corps Reserve (Retired)
Williamsburg, Virginia

CAPSTONE PRESS
a capstone imprint

Edge Books are published by Capstone Press,
1710 Roe Crest Drive, North Mankato, Minnesota 56003
www.capstonepub.com

**Library of Congress Cataloging-in-Publication Data**
Schaub, Michelle.
Vehicles of World War I / by Michelle Schaub.
pages cm.—(Edge books. War vehicles)
Includes bibliographical references and index.
Summary: "Describes various land, air, and sea vehicles used by the Central Powers
and the Allied Powers during World War I"—Provided by publisher.
Audience: Ages 8-14.
ISBN 978-1-4296-9911-2 (library binding)
ISBN 978-1-4765-3376-6 (eBook PDF)
1. Vehicles, Military—History—20th century—Juvenile literature. 2. World War,
1914–1918—Transportation—Juvenile literature. 3. World War, 1914–1918—Equipment
and supplies—Juvenile literature. I. Title.
UG615.S43 2014
940.4—dc23                                                          2013005619

**Editorial Credits**
Aaron Sautter, editor; Heidi Thompson, designer; Eric Manske, production specialist

**Photo Credits**
Alamy: Bob Masters, 8, Classic Image, 26 (bottom), INTERFOTO/History, 14b, 25b,
Mary Evans Picture Library, 11 (top), Photos 12, 5, Photos 12/Collection Bernard
Crochet, 26t, Photos 12/Oasis, 10t, Prisma Bildagentur AG/Schultz Reinhard, 16,
The Print Collector, 19b, 29t; AP Images, 17t; Corbis, 9t, 28t, Bettmann, 19t, National
Geographic Society/Boston Photo News Co, 9b, National Geographic Society/
Underwood & Underwood, 7, The Mariner's Museum, 28b; Getty Images: Hulton
Archive, 12, 22; James P. Rowan, 13b; Mary Evans Picture Library, 20b, Epic/Tallandier,
11b, Robert Hunt Library, 18b, 20t, 25t, 27b, Robert Hunt Library/© Imperial War
Museum, 21t, 27t; National Archives and Records Administration, cover, 13t; National
Museum of the Air Force, 17b; Newscom: Mirrorpix/Topical Press, 10b; U.S. Navy
photo, 24, 29b; Wikimedia, 14t, 18t, 21b, 23 (both), Mulholiant, 15

**Artistic Effects**
Shutterstock

Printed in the United States of America in Stevens Point, Wisconsin.
032012  007227WZF13

# Table of Contents

Three huge shapes rumbled through the morning fog. Heavy gunfire blazed through the air. German forces were trying to stop three British Mark IV tanks near Villers-Bretonneux, France. As the fog cleared on April 24, 1918, three giant German A7V tanks moved toward the British tanks. Tanks on both sides took heavy damage, and neither side could advance. Stalemates such as these were common during World War I (1914–1918).

The war began on June 28, 1914, when Archduke Franz Ferdinand of Austria-Hungary was **assassinated**. Austria-Hungary quickly declared war on Serbia, which it blamed for the killing. During that time many European nations were involved in different **alliances**. After Ferdinand's death, countries took sides based on those alliances. Germany backed Austria-Hungary. They were soon joined by Bulgaria and the Ottoman Empire in present-day Turkey. Together, these countries were known as the Central Powers.

**assassinate**—to murder a person who is well known or important, often for political reasons

**alliance**—an agreement between nations or groups of people to work together

Several nations came together to fight the Central Powers. France, Great Britain, Russia, and Italy joined to form the Allied Powers, or Allies. The United States later joined the Allies in 1917. Countries from around the world were soon fighting in the biggest conflict the world had ever seen.

## WAR FACT

World War I was often called the "Great War" or the "War to End All Wars." It wasn't called "World War I" at first. At that time nobody knew there would later be a second World War.

German A7V tanks fought British Mark IV tanks in the first tank versus tank battle in history.

# MILITARY ADVANCEMENTS

World War I saw a huge jump in the technology used for military vehicles. These advanced vehicles had a major impact on how battles were fought on land, in the air, and at sea. Tanks were used regularly for the first time during the war. These armored combat vehicles gave armies a strong advantage on the battlefield.

At the start of the war, airplanes were still a new invention. But as the war went on, military leaders learned that airplanes could be very useful. Throughout the war, countries built faster, more powerful military aircraft.

Until the late 1800s, ships were mostly made from wood. They also relied on sails to cross the ocean. But new warships were made from strong steel and were powered by steam engines. Submarines, with **torpedoes** and **periscopes**, also played a major role in combat.

**torpedo**—an underwater weapon that explodes when it hits a target

**periscope**—a device in a submarine that allows sailors to see what is happening above the water

## Trenches and Tanks

Both the Central Powers and Allies dug trenches to protect soldiers from enemy fire. The trenches were usually lined with barbed wire and defended by machine guns. These trenches crisscrossed much of Europe—making it nearly impossible to break through enemy lines.

Tanks were secretly developed to solve this problem. Tanks were covered in armor to protect soldiers. Their tracks helped the vehicles move through barbed wire to cross over trenches. Tanks' ability to cross enemy lines made a big difference for the Allies in the war.

**Large warships were armed with huge guns that could hit targets several miles away.**

## ···TRANSPORT VEHICLES···

When World War I began, motorized vehicles were fairly new. Armies on both sides still depended on horses for transportation. But as the war continued, military leaders saw the need for fast, armored transport and combat vehicles. To meet this need, both sides began producing land vehicles for the war effort.

# Harley-Davidson Motorcycle

Fast, nimble motorcycles were great for **reconnaissance** work and carrying messages. Many motorcycles had special sidecars equipped with machine guns. U.S. motorcycle company Harley-Davidson built thousands of motorcycles for Allied troops.

**reconnaissance**—a mission to gather information about an enemy

# Four-Wheel Drive (FWD) Trucks

Europe had few paved roads during the war. The Four-Wheel Drive Auto Company in Wisconsin supplied about half of the 16,000 FWD trucks used by Allied troops. These vehicles' engines powered all four wheels to keep the trucks from getting stuck in muddy ground. But the ride in these trucks was extremely bumpy. Some soldiers wore a special pad called a kidney belt to cushion the jarring ride.

## Horses

Both the Allied and Central Powers relied heavily on horses. Lighter horses pulled ambulance wagons, supply wagons, and small artillery. They were also used for reconnaissance missions and for carrying messages. Heavier draft horses were used to pull larger artillery.

Both sides used several million horses in the war. Some soldiers were specially trained to groom, shoe, harness, and breed horses. Like human soldiers, many horses faced illness and injury on the battlefield. These sick and wounded horses were treated in special military veterinary hospitals.

# British Motor Bus

At the start of the war, the Allies used several British double-decker buses to transport troops and supplies to the front lines. However, they were not painted with military colors at first. They were shipped to France still decorated with bright colors and advertisements. The buses later received a makeover. They were repainted with army-issue khaki paint and fitted with toolboxes and storage racks.

## Railroads

Trains provided a fast, powerful form of transportation during the war. Networks of railways stretched like a web across Europe. Military forces could quickly transport soldiers, weapons, and supplies to the front lines. Ambulance trains were also used as moving hospitals to care for wounded troops. Some ambulance trains even included an operating room.

## WAR FACT

Trains were not the only vehicles found on railways. Military forces also used rail vehicles called draisines. These small, armored vehicles looked like tiny tanks that rolled along the tracks. Draisines were used for patrolling the front lines or for scouting enemy locations.

# Open Touring Cars

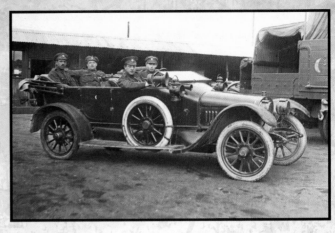

Both Allied and Central Powers officers often traveled in open-topped touring cars. At the start of the war, U.S. military cars were painted blue. They were later painted olive green when the U.S. Army changed its official colors. The 1918 Cadillac Type 57 was a popular car used to transport American officers in France.

# Ambulances

Private companies donated many cars and trucks to help support the war effort. Some of these vehicles were modified to serve as ambulances. A standard British heavy ambulance carried one driver, one attendant, and four stretchers for wounded soldiers. Many ambulances in France started out as taxis. On September 9, 1914, all the taxis in Paris were forced to transport troops to the front lines. Some of them were later turned into ambulances. A framework was added to hold stretchers for wounded troops.

# British Mark Series

The British Mark I was the first tank ever used in combat. The first shipment of Mark I tanks arrived in France in disguised crates. At first, the appearance of these 28-ton (25-metric ton) "land battleships" stunned the Germans. But the Mark I was slow, hard to drive, and it often broke down. Its slow speed made the tank an easy target for enemy fire. And its long-barreled gun often dug into the mud as it climbed over obstacles. As the war went on, British Mark tanks went through several improvements. The Mark IV had a short-barreled gun and thicker armor for better protection from enemy bullets.

## WAR FACT

The Mark V was the fastest and sturdiest tank of the Mark series. It could reach speeds of more than 4 miles (6.4 kilometers) per hour. It also had better ventilation and improved visibility for the soldiers inside.

# French Renault FT 17

The French-designed Renault FT 17 was the first tank to have a fully rotating **turret**. The turret was mounted with a machine gun that could be aimed in any direction. Renaults weighed about 6.5 tons (5.9 metric tons). Its crew was made up of a driver and a gunner. The United States, Russia, and Great Britain all used Renault FT 17s on the battlefield.

# United States M1917

The United States' first tank, the M1917, was built near the end of the war. The United States built 31 of these tanks and sent 10 to Europe. None were used in battle. However, the knowledge gained from designing the M1917 helped in creating future U.S. tank designs.

**turret**—a rotating, armored structure that holds a weapon on top of a military vehicle

# Ehrhardt E-V/4

Early armored combat vehicles like the German Ehrhardt E-V/4 offered protection from machine gun fire. But they were heavy, slow, and clumsy. The E-V/4 had a boxlike body with a small dome on top. It was armed with three machine guns and held a crew of eight to nine soldiers.

# German A7V

For most of the war, German leaders thought tanks had little value. But when Allied tanks started crashing through German lines, they soon changed their minds. The German A7V was the first and only German tank used during the war. The huge A7V held 18 men, the largest crew of any World War I tank. The tank's weapons included one large 57 mm front cannon and six smaller machine guns along the sides and back.

## Number of Tanks Produced from 1916–1918

| Year | Britain | France | Germany | Italy | U.S.A. |
|------|---------|--------|---------|-------|--------|
| 1916 | 150 | - | - | - | - |
| 1917 | 1,277 | 800 | - | - | - |
| 1918 | 1,391 | 4,000 | 20 | 6 | 84 |

# German K-Wagen

Near the end of the war, Germany began designing a giant tank that could crush enemy forces. This beastly machine was named the K-Wagen. Plans called for it to be 43 feet (13 meters) long, 20 feet (6 m) wide, and 10 feet (3 m) tall. It would have weighed 120 tons (109 metric tons). The K-Wagen would have carried four cannons and seven machine guns. And it would have held a crew of 27 soldiers. The German war ministry ordered 10 K-Wagens, but Germany surrendered to the Allies before the giant tanks were finished.

## WAR FACT

While the Allies focused on increasing the number and quality of their tanks, Germany focused on producing anti-tank weapons. The T-Gewehr was the first rifle designed to destroy armored tanks. Its bullets could pierce 0.75-inch (1.9-cm) thick armor from more than 300 feet (91 m) away.

At first, airplanes were used mostly to learn enemy locations and movement. But as the war went on, planes and pilots became more specialized. Small, nimble fighter planes were used to shoot down enemy aircraft. Large bomber planes traveled long distances to destroy enemy ground targets.

## ···ALLIED FIGHTERS···

### Nieuport 11

First used in January 1916, the Nieuport 11 was a French **biplane** fighter. It could reach speeds of 97 miles (156 km) per hour and heights of 14,765 feet (4,500 m). However, the Nieuport 11 had one major design problem—its wing structure was weak. The lower wing tended to buckle under too much stress, such as in a steep dive.

**biplane**—an early airplane with two sets of wings

# SPAD VII

In 1916 the Spad VII replaced the Nieuport as the primary fighter plane for France, Britain, and the United States. The SPAD VII was sturdier than the Nieuport planes and could dive better at high speeds. This single–seat biplane could fly up to 119 miles (192 km) per hour and reach heights of 17,500 feet (5,334 m).

# Sopwith Camel

The most famous British fighter of the war was the Sopwith Camel. It was named for the cover over the plane's twin machine guns that looked like a camel's hump. Sopwith Camels took down 1,294 enemy aircraft during the war. A naval version of the Camel was launched from battleships and the first makeshift aircraft carriers.

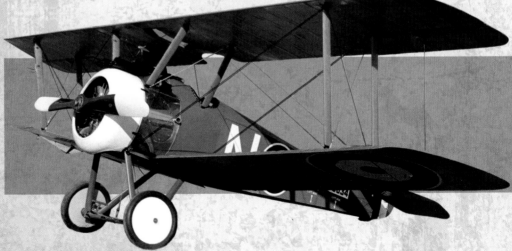

## Fokker Eindecker

At first glance, the German Fokker Eindecker wasn't very impressive. The single-seat plane could reach speeds of only 87 miles (140 km) per hour. But the Eindecker had a secret weapon. It was the first fighter plane to match machine gun fire with the rotation of the plane's propeller. German designer Anthony Fokker figured out how to time a gun's bullets so they passed between the propeller blades. This invention allowed German pilots to shoot accurately at targets without damaging the plane's propeller.

### WAR FACT

World War I fighter pilots didn't use parachutes. Parachutes were large and heavy and didn't fit well in fighter planes' small cockpits. Officers also thought parachutes tempted pilots to jump out of damaged planes instead of fighting.

## Albatros

The Albatros series of fighters were used by the highly skilled German Jasta pilots. The Albatros was the main German fighter in the April 1917 Battle of Arras, also known as "Bloody April." German pilots shot down 245 British aircraft.

# Fokker Dr.1

The most famous German airplane of the war was the Fokker Dr.1. It was flown by Baron Manfred von Richthofen, also known as the "Red Baron." Von Richthofen was the top German fighter pilot of the war. Most Fokker Dr.1 fighters were painted green and blue. But von Richthofen had his plane painted bright red.

# Aviatik D.I

For much of the war, the Austro-Hungarian Air Service flew German planes. But in 1917, Austria-Hungary designed and produced the Aviatik D.I. The plane was nicknamed "The Berg Fighter" after its designer, Julius von Berg. The Austro-Hungarian Air Service used the Berg Fighter mainly as an escort to guide and protect other planes. Pilots still flew German-designed fighters for their superior combat performance.

# Sikorsky IM

Powered by four engines, the Russian-designed Sikorsky IM was a huge plane for its time. It could carry up to 12 crewmembers and more than 1,760 pounds (800 kg) of bombs. By the end of the war, these big bombers had flown more than 400 missions and dropped 72 tons (65 metric tons) of bombs.

# Voisin III

The first genuine bomber used in combat was the French-built Voisin III. The Voisin's tough steel frame helped it withstand extreme weather conditions. Early in the war, the Voisin was used to attack German **zeppelin hangars**. Voisin bombers also targeted German factories that made gas weapons.

**zeppelin**—a large oval-shaped airship with a rigid frame

**hangar**—a large sheltered area where aircraft are parked and maintained

# Airco DH4

The Airco DH4 was a British light day bomber. It held up to 460 pounds (209 kg) of bombs. Four DH4 bombers were credited with sinking the German U-boat UB 12 in August 1918. In the same month, another DH4 shot down a German zeppelin.

# Caproni Bomber

The Italian-designed Caproni was used regularly for raids against Austro-Hungarian military targets. A later version was adapted to transport wounded soldiers. After the war, many Caproni bombers were refitted as passenger planes.

## German Zeppelin

At the start of the war, Germany's main air weapon was the zeppelin. These airships were often more than 500 feet (152 m) long and could carry thousands of pounds of bombs. Zeppelins terrorized the skies over London and Paris. They often approached silently at night to drop their deadly cargo on civilian targets.

## Flying Torch

Zeppelins were made with a lightweight metal frame and covered with a fabric skin. These giant airships were lifted into the air by hydrogen gas. At first, zeppelins were hard to attack because they could climb higher than early fighter planes. But as the Allies designed new planes with more powerful engines, zeppelins became vulnerable. Pilots shot special flammable bullets at the German airships. These bullets would light the hydrogen gas, turning the zeppelin into a giant flying torch.

# Gotha Bomber

German Gotha bombers were the most important Central Powers bombers of the war. The Gotha could climb to 21,325 feet (6,500 m). Most early Allied planes could not reach this height. This advantage allowed Gotha bombers to carry out many daytime raids. The G.III model could carry up to 880 pounds (399 kg) of bombs.

# Zeppelin-Staaken R.VI

At more than 72 feet (22 m) long, the Zeppelin-Staaken R.VI was one of the largest aircraft used in the war. It was armed with four to six machine guns and could carry two 2,200-pound (1,000-kg) bombs. This giant bomber assisted Gotha bombers with raids on London, England and Paris, France. It also bombed targets in Russia, Poland, and other countries in Eastern Europe.

Battleships were the largest and most powerful warships for both the Allied and Central Powers navies. Both sides supported their fleets with a variety of specialized ships. Submarines also were used regularly for the first time during World War I.

## ···BATTLESHIPS···

### USS *Nevada*

In 1918 the USS *Nevada* and her sister ship, the USS *Oklahoma*, sailed to the European war zone in the North Atlantic. Their job was to patrol sea routes and protect

Allied supply ships from German attack. These battleships carried ten 14-inch (35.6-cm) guns and 21 5-inch (13-cm) guns.

# Queen Elizabeth Ships

The Queen Elizabeth class was Britain's top line of battleships. These battleships were the first to be fueled by oil instead of coal. Queen Elizabeth class ships were well armed with eight 15-inch (38-cm) guns, sixteen 6-inch (15-cm) guns, two 3-inch (7.6-cm) guns, and four torpedo tubes. All of the Queen Elizabeth class ships, except the *Queen Elizabeth* itself, took part in the Battle of Jutland in 1916.

## The Battle of Jutland

The Battle of Jutland was the largest and most famous sea battle of World War I. The German High Seas Fleet planned to trap the British Grand Fleet in the North Sea. But the British learned of this plan by capturing secret German codes. On May 31, 1916, the British had their own warships waiting for the attack. By the next day, 14 British and 11 German ships were sunk. Britain lost more ships, but Germany's fleet was more heavily affected. Britain kept control of the North Sea.

## German König Ships

The most powerful German warships at the start of the war were in the König class. These battleships were heavily armed with a total of 34 large guns. They led the German fleet during the famous Battle of Jutland. During the battle the *König*, *Grosser Kurfürst*, and *Markgraf* were heavily damaged, but all survived.

# British Light Cruisers

British light cruisers, like the HMS *Dublin*, were multi-purpose warships. Cruisers were used for patrolling, raiding, supporting battleships, and leading destroyer fleets. One of the *Dublin*'s duties was to protect the battleship HMS *Queen Elizabeth* during attacks on forts on the coast of Turkey.

# German Light Cruisers

The Germans also built light cruisers, but they were bigger and slower than British cruisers. The SMS *Mainz* and other German light cruisers fought in the first major sea battle of the war, the Battle of Heligoland Bight on August 28, 1914. The *Mainz* was sunk by British light cruisers in the battle.

# Destroyers

Destroyers were used to defend larger ships against smaller vessels like mine-laying boats. The HMS *Lance* carried three 4-inch (10-cm) guns, one 40 mm antiaircraft gun, and two torpedo tubes. On August 4, 1914, the *Lance* fired the first shots of any British ship in the war. The *Lance* also helped sink the first German ship of the war, the *Konigin Luise*, which had been laying mines in the North Sea.

# Monitors

Monitors were small warships that carried one or two large guns. Monitors were not very fast or well armored. They were not meant for sea combat. They were instead used to give close support to land troops.

# German U-boat

The German Navy dominated undersea warfare with its well-built U-boats. Short for "undersea boats," these submarines were feared by the Allies. Germany had built more than 360 U-boats by the end of the war. The subs sank thousands of Allied ships over the course of the war.

## Sinking the *Lusitania*

The most famous naval attack of the war occurred on May 7, 1915, near the coast of Ireland. When the German submarine U-20 spotted the British passenger ship RMS *Lusitania*, it fired one torpedo. The torpedo blew a hole in the side of the ship. Shortly after, ammunition carried by the *Lusitania* exploded and blasted through the ship's hull. The *Lusitania* sank in just 18 minutes. Nearly 1,200 people died. More than 120 of the victims were U.S. citizens. This attack was a major reason the United States decided to enter the war.

# British E-class

British E-class submarines were used to target enemy warships and to block merchant ships carrying supplies to Germany. On October 11, 1915, the E-19 sank five merchant ships in one day. The ships had been carrying tons of iron ore meant to build ships and weapons for the Central Powers.

# United States K-class subs

The first U.S. subs to arrive in European waters were in the K-class. These subs were sent by the U.S. Navy to help combat Germany's U-boats. K-class subs could travel faster than British or German subs, but were not as well armed.

# Glossary

**alliance** (uh-LY-uhns)—an agreement between nations or groups of people to work together

**artillery** (ar-TI-luhr-ee)—cannons and other large guns used during battles

**assassinate** (us-SASS-uh-nate)—to murder a person who is well known or important, often for political reasons

**biplane** (BY-plane)—an airplane with two sets of wings, one above the other

**hangar** (HANG-ur)—a large sheltered area where aircraft are parked and maintained

**periscope** (PAIR-uh-skope)—a device used in submarines that allows sailors to see what is happening above the water

**reconnaissance** (ree-KAH-nuh-suhnss)—a mission to gather information about an enemy

**stalemate** (STAYL-mayt)—a situation in which neither side of opposing forces can win

**torpedo** (tor-PEE-doh)—an underwater missile used to blow up a target

**trench** (TRENCH)—a long, narrow ditch dug in the ground to serve as shelter from enemy fire or attack

**turret** (TUR-it)—a rotating, armored structure that holds a weapon on top of a military vehicle

**zeppelin** (ZEP-uh-lin)—a large oval-shaped airship with a rigid frame; zeppelins are named for their inventor, Count Ferdinand von Zeppelin

# Read More >

**Adams, Simon.** *World War I.* DK Eyewitness Books. New York: Dorling Kindersley, 2007.

**Fein, Eric.** *Weapons, Gear, and Uniforms of World War I.* Equipped for Battle. Mankato, Minn.: Capstone Press, 2012.

**Perritano, John.** *World War I.* America at War. New York: Franklin Watts, 2010.

# Internet Sites >

FactHound offers a safe, fun way to find Internet sites related to this book. All of the sites on FactHound have been researched by our staff.

Here's all you do:

Visit *www.facthound.com*

Type in this code: 9781429699112

**Super-cool stuff!** Check out projects, games and lots more at **www.capstonekids.com**

# Index >